Original title:

The Tropics, the Sky, the Sea

Copyright © 2025 Creative Arts Management OÜ
All rights reserved.

Author: Colin Harrington
ISBN HARDBACK: 978-1-80581-543-3
ISBN PAPERBACK: 978-1-80581-070-4
ISBN EBOOK: 978-1-80581-543-3

Lullabies of the Lotus Blooms

In a pond where ducks traipse,
Lotus buds wear silly capes.
They sing songs, so wild and free,
With frog choirs playing in harmony.

When evening falls, fireflies sway,
They twirl around in a bright ballet.
While turtles nod in a sleepy trance,
Hoping for a midnight dance.

Radiant Echoes of Distal Shores

On sandy islands, crabs stand tall,
Dancing sideways at every call.
Seagulls squawk a comic tune,
While sunbathers roast like marshmallows soon.

Breezy whispers of coconut dreams,
Wave-laughs bubble like frothy streams.
With no schedule, just fun to find,
Every hour feels unconfined.

The Luminescence of Evening Tide

Beneath the waves, fish wear shades,
Kicking back in our ocean glades.
Starfish and squid partake in jest,
In a water world, they're all dressed best.

As twilight casts its winking glow,
Crabs exchange secrets like old pros.
While shells gossip like chatty friends,
And laughter echoes, never ends.

Coconuts and Clouds

Coconuts wear goofy grins,
As monkeys plot their playful sins.
A brisk wind adds a chatty sound,
While palm trees sway, they joke around.

Clouds drape down like fluffy pies,
Hiding secrets and little sighs.
With a splash, the waters cheer,
For every giggle that we hear.

Serengeti of Echoes

In a land where the sun sticks like gum,
Monkeys swing and make quite the hum.
Parrots squawk with a colorful boast,
Claiming to be the witty host!

Lizards lounge like they own the place,
Sunbathing in a bright, warm embrace.
With a wink from a cheeky gecko,
The world's a stage for this great show!

Bursting Blossoms and Briny Depths

Flowers giggle in the humid air,
Dancing wildly, without a care.
While crabs in tuxedos scuttle about,
Shaking claws and singing out loud!

Seashells hold secrets and snickers, too,
As fish play cards with a wink and a moo.
Tropical breezes blow jokes your way,
Try to catch them—oh, what a play!

Ribbons of Dawn

Morning wakes like an over-caffeinated kid,
A splash of colors it can't quite rid.
Waves tickle the shore with a mischievous grin,
Spilling jokes like confetti, where to begin?

Sandy toes prance in the golden light,
While dolphins burst forth in pure delight.
The sun can be silly, with rays that poke fun,
Reminding us all, life's a game to be won!

Translucent Horizons

Clouds tumble like jesters in the blue,
Casting shadows that play peek-a-boo.
A kite gets tangled in a laugh-off duel,
While kids chase dreams—oh, how they rule!

The breeze unfurls stories, like sails on a ship,
Each gust whispers jokes—oh, take a trip!
When dusk arrives, wearing a pun-filled coat,
We'll dance with the stars, on this merry boat!

A Stray Feather on the Breeze

A feather floats, lost in flight,
Dancing with laughs under bright sunlight.
Chasing a seagull who thinks it's grand,
Swirling like mischief in a child's hand.

Tickled by jokes from the palm trees,
While coconuts nod with perfect ease.
A breeze teases hats on the heads of fools,
While flip-flops stumble like mischievous mules.

Beyond the Surf and Sand

Waves whisper tales to the sandy shore,
Where crabs throw parties, but nobody's sure.
They scuttle about with shells on their backs,
Wearing sunglasses, avoiding the cracks.

Frogs on loungers sip on bug juice,
While starfish gossip, calling a truce.
Seashells collect secrets, tell a few lies,
As the tide rolls in with a wink in its eyes.

Hues of a Silent Morning

A parrot squawks at a sleepy sun,
As it yawns and stretches, it's day just begun.
Colors explode like confetti in flight,
While the sea chuckles, glinting with light.

Bamboo sways, sharing a giggle or two,
While bright flowers gossip in candied hue.
The starfish grins as it wiggles its toes,
Underneath waves where the laughter just flows.

Shores of Colorful Reveries

Here, the sand plays tricks, shifting like dreams,
While jellyfish waltz as the sunlight gleams.
Octopuses juggle with arms open wide,
Catching passes from dolphins who glide.

Palm trees hold birthday bashes all day,
With coconuts, juice, and a wind-up display.
Yet, beware of the gulls, they steal your fry,
As laughter erupts from the clouds up high.

Salted Breezes and Tropical Serenades

In a hammock I sway, oh what a delight,
Eating coconuts by day, rum by night.
A parrot squawks loudly, claims it knows best,
While I stifle a laugh, feeling quite blessed.

The sun makes me sticky, like melted ice cream,
And the surf's funny rhythm flows like a dream.
Seagulls steal fries from a child by the shore,
While I chuckle watching them squawk for some more.

Fragments of Paradise

Flip-flops flip-flop as I trip on the sand,
I'm searching for treasures, but just found a hand.
The crab nearby dances, showing off its flair,
While I hop around, pretending I don't care.

A breeze plays my hair like a silly old tune,
As I chat with a shell, feeling over the moon.
Laughter erupts as a wave takes a dive,
My shorts soaked and dripping, yet I feel so alive!

Dancing Palms and Moonlit Tides

The palm trees are waltzing, or maybe they're drunk,
With coconuts falling, it's a nutty old funk.
A crab wears a grass skirt, preparing for flair,
While I slide on the sand, my dance quite a scare.

The moon's so bright, it could light up a cave,
While I sip on a drink, feeling oh so brave.
A fish flops beside me, like it wants to dance,
But all it can do is give the sand a chance!

Mariner's Reverie

With a hat made of bamboo and shades made of wine,
I sail on my floatie, feeling just fine.
The gulls yell, 'Ahoy!' as they dive for a snack,
While I grin and pretend that the ship's not a quack.

Fish greet me with bubbles, all smiles and no frowns,
As I wave at the dolphins in my upside-down towns.
Life's a comic strip under the sunny patrol,
With sunburned laughter playing the lead role!

Shimmering Depths

Beneath the waves, the fish all dance,
In tiny hats, they take their chance.
A hermit crab sings with great flair,
While seahorses twirl without a care.

A dolphin wears shades, looking quite cool,
Pretending to be the world's first pool.
With laughter bubbles filling the spray,
We float on our backs and drift away.

Echoes of Paradise

Palm trees whisper secrets in the breeze,
While parrots shout like they've got degrees.
Monkeys swing by, throwing coconuts round,
Apparently, they've got no use for the ground.

The sunset paints oranges, pinks, and blues,
While crabs in tuxedos discuss the news.
With laughter echoing through the warm night,
Even the stars burst out in delight.

Breezes Through Bougainvillea

Flowers wave hello, with colors so bright,
They giggle as bees hover, taking a bite.
A lizard in shades strikes a pose on a wall,
While I sit and sip from my coconut so tall.

The breeze tells stories of sunburnt woes,
As I plan my escape from all pesky toes.
But oh look, a toucan with flair can't be beat,
Wearing its beak like the ultimate treat.

Twilight Reflections

At dusk, the flamingos gather in sync,
Discussing the best shade of pink that they think.
While fish in the shallows pretend they're a band,
Making music with bubbles just as they planned.

The moon sneaks up with a cheeky little grin,
While crabs start waltzing, resembling a spin.
With laughter ringing through this playful parade,
Tomorrow's another day, with more fun to be made.

A Radiant Horizon Unfurled

Bright oranges and yellows perceive,
Fishes swim by, trying to leave.
A floating hat sails on by,
While sunbathers sneeze and sigh.

The seagulls laugh at a man's flip,
He drops his sandwich, a slippery trip.
Waves crash down with a bubbly cheer,
As sunscreen artists draw with no fear.

Coconuts drop with a thud so loud,
While crabs dance about, feeling proud.
Tanned toes in the air, a sight to see,
Next to a guy with a blender for tea!

Song of the Moonlit Bay

The moon peeks down, a silver coin,
While fishermen dance, their lives to join.
Splash and giggle from waves so bold,
A mermaid hums as stories unfold.

Tangled in seaweed, a tale goes awry,
A dolphin's grin seems to wink and sigh.
Shady young sharks in a minnow parade,
Promising riches from underwater trade.

The night is alive as crickets play,
With the tides as jokes twist and sway.
Stars blink down at a monkey show,
Making faces, putting on a glow.

Lies Beneath the Surface

Coral castles hide lost dreams,
While octopuses plan with scheming beams.
Fish in bow ties swim with flair,
Creating chaos, an underwater fair.

A sea cucumber trip slips and twirls,
While squirty squids throw slimy pearls.
Tiny crabs act as a secret spies,
Whispering tales of epic fries.

Bubbles float like thoughts from the past,
As eel jokes swim, unsurpassed.
A turtle laughs, 'It's all in good jest!'
While tides tickle, tickling's the best!

Aqua Horizons and Clouded Dreams

Splashing waves chase clouds away,
While flip-flops have an aerial ballet.
Buried treasure in sand so wide,
With hooting parrots, can't let it slide.

A cocktail claims to cure blunders,
But it just serves up fruity wonders.
The sunbathers plot a sunscreen scheme,
While jellyfish dance, making them scream!

Shady umbrellas tilt like grand pals,
As everyone jokes about their wild swells.
Starfish hitchhikers in bright, bold hues,
Waiting for swim trunks, or silly cues!

When Islands Drift to Dream

When isles float like jelly beans,
Brought forth by cheeky streams.
Palm trees dance, oh what a sight,
Under the moon, they sway at night.

Crabs with shades and sandals too,
Playing limbo, just for you.
Bananas wear their brightest smiles,
As lizards try out fancy styles.

Reflection in Clear Waters

Look down deep, what do you see?
A fish in plaid, swimming with glee.
Mermaids giggling, brushing their hair,
While turtles pose for selfies, beware!

Ripples giggle, they splash and sway,
Water's a dance floor, come out and play.
In costumes made from seaweed bright,
The ocean's a party, both day and night.

Whispering Winds and Glistening Sands

Winds carry tales from sandy shores,
Where crabs hold court and debate galores.
A whispering breeze with secrets to share,
Tickles our toes, it's quite the affair.

Footprints fade like a bad song,
The sun beaming down, tu-tu-ta-ta- wrong!
Coconut cups and laughs that resound,
In this mirthful realm, joy knows no bounds.

Oceanic Embrace

Embraced by waves that giggle and tease,
Salty hugs that come with the breeze.
Dolphins show off their latest tricks,
While seagulls swoop down for snack attacks.

Floating on rafts made of dreams,
Life's a comedy, bursting at the seams.
Shells tell stories of jest and cheer,
In this watery world, fun's always near.

Palette of the Paradise River

A splash of color in the day,

A fish that sings, oh what a play!

Coconuts rolling, chasing the breeze,

Even crabs try to dance with ease.

The water's warm, a silly sight,

A turtle in shades of disco light.

With every wave, the jellyfish grin,

While the parrots squawk, 'Let the games begin!'

The Voice of Distant Callings

A parrot yells, 'Hey, look at me!'

A monkey throws its lunch at a tree.

A distant horn blows, where's the parade?

Here comes a goat, with a hat, homemade!

Fluttering bugs in a waltzing spree,

The sun beats down like a hot cup of tea.

A toucan talks, in a language of cheer,

'Come for the fun, stay for the beer!'

Under the Wild Canopy

Bananas dangle, a swing on a vine,

A sloth takes a nap, oh, how divine!

With giggles and wiggles, a monkey troupe,

Hiding behind leaves, plotting a scoop.

The colors clash like kids on a ride,

While turtles attempt to surf with pride.

Between the branches, laughter does sway,

As a snake tries to join in the play.

Shades of a Forgotten Cove

In the shade where the palm fronds sway,

Laughter echoes of yesterday.

Creatures scurry, play hide and seek,

While crabs declare, 'We're not so bleak!'

A starfish dreams of modeling fame,

While a beach ball rolls, oh what a game!

With sunburnt noses and giggling sounds,

Joy can be found in these leafy grounds.

Beneath a Canopy of Stars

Under twinkling lights so bright,
The crabs dance left, then take flight.
A fish named Fred wore a top hat,
Said, 'Join my band, but please don't chat!'

The moon winks down with a cheeky gleam,
While coconut drinks spill like a dream.
Parrots gossip, squawking in fun,
'Who'd have thought the stars could run?'

Currents of Eden

In a whirlpool of laughter and glee,
A dolphin joked, 'Come swim with me!'
Octopus wearing polka-dot shoes,
Said, 'I'm the best in these lovely blues!'

Turtles race, but it's quite unclear,
Who's the fastest—none volunteer!
Jellyfish light up, a neon delight,
Claiming their glow makes them so bright.

Sunlit Waves and Dappled Shade

Seagulls swoop down with a playful tease,
Searching for snacks with the greatest of ease.
A snail on the shore had dreams of a race,
But just turned around, 'Let's chill in this place.'

The sand gets hot, but who really cares?
Mermaids joke about untangling hairs.
'Let's craft a hat from this driftwood nearby,
And pretend we're the kings of the sunburnt sky!'

Celestial Embrace of the Isles

Stars play hide and seek with the breeze,
While iguanas lounge beneath the trees.
'What's that smell?' asks a curious parrot,
'Just my lunchbox, mind your own carrot!'

The tides tell tales from a watery past,
Where sea cucumbers can sing quite fast.
A fisherman's net, filled with giggles and grins,
'Caught a good time, let the party begin!'

Lush Echoes of the Heart

Bananas in bow ties, dancing with glee,
Parrots sing love songs, sipping iced tea.
Coconuts chuckle, as palm trees sway,
Here in this paradise, we frolic all day.

Flip-flops are flying, like fish on a hook,
Seagulls drop treats, what a fun little nook.
Every wave whispers secrets of cheer,
Sunshine's our buddy, and it's always near.

A Symphony of Blue and Green

Lemonade rivers, with sprinkles on top,
Fishes in top hats, they twirl and they hop.
Turtles in shades, sunbathing with pride,
Every moment here, it's a quirky ride.

Jellyfish jiggle, like jiggly desserts,
Octopuses play cards, oh how it confers!
Colorful critters join in the parade,
This underwater dance, never shall we trade.

Secrets of the Coral Depths

In a world of bubbles, where laughter is deep,
Clownfish do stand-up, while others just peep.
Mermaids with smartphones, take selfies in style,
Ocean's the circus, come watch for a while.

Corals are giggling, with polka-dot flair,
Starfish with mustaches, float round without care.
Every fin wiggles, with tales to impart,
Secrets that linger, beneath sandy art.

Solstice of the Sunlit Reefs

Bikinis with stripes, like candy canes cheer,
Seashells whisper jokes for all who can hear.
The sun plays peekaboo, casting bright rays,
While crabs dance the limbo, in whimsical ways.

Flip-flop contests, who can throw far?
Seagulls are judges, they giggle and spar.
Surfers ride rainbows, in the foamy parade,
A fest of delight, this bliss never fades.

Tide and Twilight

In the evening glow, so bright,
Stars blink with glee, what a sight!
A crab does the cha-cha, quite spry,
While shadows dance, oh my, oh my!

Jellyfish float with a grin,
Mimicking folks who've had gin.
The waves whisper secrets, oh dear,
Like gossiping friends, can you hear?

A fish in a bowtie swims by,
As seagulls join in, oh, they fly high.
Sand castles crumble in laughter,
As the tide rolls in, seeking after.

Now the moon wears a silly hat,
While a pufferfish struts like a brat.
With each wave comes a chuckle and cheer,
Night's a party, let's all raise a beer!

Celestial Sojourn

In a hammock swaying with flair,
A dog dreams of chasing rare air.
Clouds parade like kings, no doubt,
A butterfly joins for the route.

Coconuts giggle, what a jest,
As sunbeams poke, a witty quest.
A parrot cracks jokes, quite absurd,
Echoing laughter, how it stirred!

With starfish doing the limbo dance,
And crabs in tuxedos, what a chance!
The breeze plays tunes on its flute,
While dancing leaves wiggle, so cute.

A moonbeam shows off its new suit,
While gulls play tag, so resolute.
Eclipses wink and cause a ruckus,
What a ride on this cosmic circus!

Aquamarine Journeys

Waves crash like laughter, so splashy,
Surfboards zoom past, oh, they're flashy!
A dolphin's flipping with delight,
As seaweed tickles, oh, what a sight!

Sea turtles sport shades, feeling grand,
While jellyfish take charge of the band.
The ocean's a stage where creatures play,
With sea cucumbers leading the way!

An octopus juggles, watch him go,
As crabs sidestep in a row, oh so slow.
The seashells whisper tales of the deep,
While fish wear bow ties to their sheep!

Starfish flip and do the twist,
As sea urchins cheer, they can't resist.
With every swell, the laughter grows,
In this watery world, fun overflows!

Solstice Reverie

The sun wakes up with a goofy grin,
As beach balls roll like they're in spin!
Sand scoops tacos for a feast,
While crabs debate who's the least.

A hammock swings in a twisty flair,
As sunscreen fights the salty air.
Palm trees gossip about the breeze,
While flip-flops march with joyful ease.

Kites swoop low, chasing a tale,
While snails debate which path will prevail.
The sun dip dances, what a sight,
As ice cream cones melt in delight!

With laughter echoing in the night,
The air hums tunes, everything's right.
A firefly winks with a playful cheer,
In this reverie, fun's always near!

Tidal Serenades

Waves bounce like an overgrown kid,
Crabs perform a funny little jig.
Seagulls cackle, they spy the fries,
While fish below hide from the spies.

Shells wear hats like they're on a spree,
Starfish cheer, 'Come dance with me!'
Sandcastles lean, it's a wobbly race,
As the tide giggles, 'Let's pick up the pace!'

Laughter echoes, the beaches play,
Watermelon smiles brighten the day.
Surfboards glide with a silly sway,
Chasing the sun until it's time to play.

Colors of an Island Sky

Clouds are marshmallows, piled so high,
A turtle waves as he swims by.
Parrots gossip about the breeze,
Turning the trees into a tease.

Dancers swirl in a limbo line,
Twinkling stars drop in just to shine.
Balloons float up, with silly faces,
While the sunset plays in vibrant races.

Chickens cluck their own parade,
Stepping lightly, they're not afraid.
Bananas laugh as they split apart,
In this crazy world, it's an art!

Windswept Shores and Solstice Skies

Kites soar high, with tails so bold,
A beach ball bounces like it's gold.
Wind chimes jingle in a twisty dance,
As crabs hold a very clumsy stance.

The sun takes a dip, just for fun,
While dolphins plan their next big run.
Waves whisper secrets, oh so sly,
And the sand giggles as they fly by.

Palm trees sway, wearing silly hats,
As iguanas yap, "Oh, how about that?"
Coconuts tumble, they like to play,
A funny beach, where it's always a day!

The Dance of Creatures Below

Bubbles rise with a comical pop,
Fish wiggle their fins; they can't stop!
Octopus plays hide and seek with glee,
While a crab says, "Why not chase me?"

Eels do the twist, and seaweed sways,
As the starfish hums in playful ways.
Jellyfish float like balloons in the blue,
While the clownfish tells jokes for you!

A anglerfish shines, like a disco light,
Setting the dance floor a little too tight.
Underwater laughter fills the sea,
In this underwater party, come join me!

Whispers of Palm Fronds

Beneath the swaying fan, they dance,
A curious bug just took a chance.
He buzzed around with quite the flair,
And tangled up in coconut hair.

The monkeys laugh, they swing and tease,
While sipping juice from giant breeze.
A parrot squawks, a raucous jest,
And leaves all gathered for a fest!

A crab with shoes, he struts so proud,
His tiny friends all gathered 'roud.
They throw a party, dance in sand,
While dreams of piña coladas planned.

In shadows deep, a lizard grins,
As sunburnt tourists trip on spins.
With goofy hats and frozen drinks,
They giggle loud, and nobody thinks.

Horizon's Embrace

A sun-drenched beach, so wide and bright,
Seagulls argue over snack delight.
The waves rush in with frothy cheer,
And tickle toes, like whispers near.

Two kids build castles, grand and tall,
Anticipating a muddy fall.
With buckets dumped, they scream and squeal,
While sandcastles flee from waves' appeal.

A dog runs wild, digs with a grin,
Uncovering treasures lost within.
He finds a flip-flop, snatches fame,
As dad just sighs, and calls his name.

As daylight fades, the sun gets shy,
They count the stars, a pizza pie.
With laughter echoing in the night,
They dance with shadows, oh what a sight!

Ocean's Serenade

A fish in shades of bright maroon,
Sings serenades, a bubbly tune.
He flops about, a silly dance,
While seaweed sways in its own prance.

A clam's shy smile, it opens slow,
As shells around begin to glow.
With pearls that sparkle, they make a wish,
To sip on drinks and feast on fish.

Crabs in tuxedos, wingtip shoes,
On evening strolls, they roam, they cruise.
They tip their hats, all in good fun,
Declaring, 'This beach life has begun!'

A dolphin leaps, a splashy break,
He tells a joke that makes them shake.
The ocean's floor, a stage so grand,
For antics played in grains of sand.

Celestial Waters

Balloons afloat, they drift and sway,
In gentle breezes through the fray.
A child points up and shouts with glee,
'Look, a whale's tail!'—oh, that's just me.

Stars wink on down, like tiny eyes,
While fireflies admire in surprise.
A jellyfish floats, looking for fame,
Telling a tale of the beach's game.

The moon takes notes on all the fun,
While crickets chirp, the night's begun.
A starfish laughs at a daring bet,
Who can jump over? Not a chance yet!

With each splash, the world looks bright,
As stories swirl into the night.
In this wild dance where we all play,
The curtains close on another day!

Gentle Swells and Golden Sands

Waves wiggle like a happy snake,
Dancing shells, the ocean's flake.
Sand stuck to toes, a gritty snack,
Seagulls squawking, popping a whack.

With each tide, a new sea toy,
A floating bottle, a plastic joy.
Kids scream, while parents nap,
That's the life, a sunny trap!

Flip-flops flying in the breeze,
Sunscreen battles, oh what a tease!
Beach balls bouncing, laughter loud,
Sandcastles built, then wrecked by proud.

At sunset's glow, they gather near,
Cracking jokes with fruity beer.
Laughter echoes, as sun dips down,
Beach life's a swirl, a merry clown!

Nature's Vivid Palette

Colors burst like fireworks bright,
Painted birds in morning light.
A butterfly with socks on right,
Blooping bees, all in flight!

Coconuts wearing shades of cool,
Palm trees sway, doing the fool.
Lime-green lizards sneak a peek,
Cockatoos squawk, their beaks do squeak.

Mangoes roll like tiny balls,
Tasting sweet, on tree top stalls.
Squirrels dance in vibrant banter,
Nature's jokes, oh what a canter!

The world blooms with goofy cheer,
As creatures frolic far and near.
Colors clash with joyous glee,
A canvas wild, just let it be!

Beneath the Endless Canopy

Leaves rustle tales of monkey prank,
Swinging high on a leafy plank.
Frogs in tuxedos croak a tune,
Chasing bugs beneath the moon.

Dappled light dances on the ground,
Where giggling flowers twirl around.
A chameleon plays hide and seek,
While parrots gossip, oh so cheek!

Dripping rain like a silly shower,
Washing off the sun's last power.
Each droplet's like a playful tease,
Nature's giggle, carried by the breeze.

Under branches, life's a game,
Every creature knows its name.
As night falls, the fun won't cease,
With stars above, it's pure caprice!

Melodies of Misty Sunsets

Evening's glow, a goofy smirk,
As crickets start their twilight work.
Catch the breeze, it's tickling toes,
While fireflies put on a show!

The horizon blushes, orange and pink,
As dolphins dive, and seagulls wink.
A coconut smooths its curly hair,
While the ocean hums a gentle flair.

Slowly, shadows stretch and tease,
Whispers of waves bring warmth and ease.
Jokes echo in the balmy air,
Laughter bounces everywhere.

As stars pop out like silly sprites,
The moon giggles, thinking of nights.
In this waltz of colors bright,
Every heart dances, pure delight!

Horizon Kisses

A bird in a hat took flight,
Sipped lemonade from a coconut bright.
Seagulls played leapfrog with the sun,
While crabs danced around, oh what fun!

A dolphin with shades did a flip,
While a fish tried to join the trip.
The beach was a party, no doubt,
With sun-soaked fun and laughter about.

The sand wore flip-flops, it seemed,
Wiggling toes while everyone dreamed.
A pineapple wearing a crown,
Said, "Why not dance? Let's not frown!"

With laughter as waves crash and play,
The horizon smiles in its own way.
So join this jamboree at our spot,
Where silliness blooms and laughter is hot!

Sails and Sunbeams

A boat made of jelly, what a sight!
Floated along, it was quite a delight.
With sails made of candy, oh so sweet,
And lollipops swirling beneath with each beat.

The captain was a parrot, quite the charmer,
Barking orders while doing a farmer.
Fish flipped with giggles in tight little rows,
While the jelly boat wobbled, but nobody knows.

Clouds tossed confetti from the azure above,
As sunbeams disco, oh how they shove!
"It's a party!" they shouted, "who's gonna take lead?
Let's toast to the jelly and the candy we need!"

A whale with a trumpet joined in the sound,
Creating a symphony above and around.
With laughter and joy on this absurd spree,
Sails and sunbeams made life feel free!

The Echo of Lapping Waters

Once there was a fish with a big ol' grin,
Who started a rumor that told fishy tales of sin.
The waves giggled back, giving splashes of cheer,
As minnows recited rhymes we could hear.

A crab threw a party on the soft sand,
With snacks consisting of seaweed hand.
They danced to the rhythm of the moonlight's glow,
While starfish were playing, putting on a show.

Laughter echoed in ripples at dusk,
With each splash of water, it felt like a husk.
The mermaids chimed in with tunes that were sly,
As dolphins busted moves, oh my!

"Let's toast to the waves and the bubbles they bring!"
Said a starfish with shades, ready to swing.
The echo of lapping brought joy with glee,
As all joined the laughter, just absurdity!

Kaleidoscope of the Wild

In a jungle of laughter and whimsy galore,
Chameleons strutted in colors that soar.
With each silly slip, they turned bright and bold,
In the dance of the bizarre, watch the stories unfold!

A monkey in a tutu twirled like a champ,
While frogs in tuxedos formed quite the camp.
Crickets played tambourines, chasing away woes,
While butterflies giggled in colorful clothes.

Parrots threw confetti, squawking with glee,
As flowers sang duets with voices like tea.
"Let's start a club!" shouted a raccoon in style,
"Where fun is the rule and laughter's the file!"

So in this wild haven of joyous delight,
Creatures embraced a rhythm so bright.
In a kaleidoscope dance that never feels stale,
Join the giggle parade, let's set sail!

A Canvas of Lush Green

In a jungle thick with zest,
Monkeys swing, they never rest.
Parrots squawk a silly tune,
Dancing under the bright moon.

Lizards wear their finest suits,
Chasing bugs in fancy boots.
Frogs croak jokes, a ribbit jest,
Nature's humor at its best.

Coconuts drop down like rain,
Laughing squirrels drive me insane.
Hammocks sway with a gentle grin,
While iguanas play a violin.

Flowers bloom with vibrant cheer,
A colorful jester's atmosphere.
Under leaves, where shadows twirl,
Nature's jesters spin and whirl.

The Breath of the Ocean

Waves crash down like a feathery sigh,
Clams clink shells, shouting hi!
Starfish giggle on the sand,
Tickled by the ocean's hand.

Seagulls steal snacks with a dive,
Chasing crumbs, they feel alive.
Crabs do the cha-cha on the shore,
Pinch and dance, they ask for more!

Surfers wobble, splash, and thrash,
Balancing like they're in a clash.
A dolphin jumps with a playful twist,
Flipping through the air, can't be missed!

Beach umbrellas spin a tale,
As kids' laughter rides the gale.
In bubbles, merry dreams arise,
Where every dip is a fun surprise.

Soaring Through Sunlit Waters

Flipping fish flash up like light,
Jumping high, they giggle bright.
A whale sings a splashy song,
Its jolly notes echo along.

Surfers slip, and seaweed clings,
While turtles wear warm winter things.
Playful dolphins race for fun,
Riding waves beneath the sun.

A buoy bobs with cheerful chat,
Determined craft keeps calling 'hat!'
Mermaids laugh in shimmering sprays,
Casting jokes in swirling bays.

Every ripple tells a jest,
Water's humor is the best.
With foam and frolic, let's embark,
Splashing joy from dawn to dark.

Tapestry of Light and Wave

Painted skies in shades so bold,
Puns of clouds like stories told.
They shaped a cow that floats on by,
And ducks that sail beneath a pie.

Sunsets giggle, turn to paste,
Colors swirl without a haste.
As fireflies dance in twilight's glow,
Winking smiles from nature's show.

Nighttime hums a lullaby,
While laughter twinkles from the sky.
A shooting star makes fun of time,
Racing dreams in a cosmic rhyme.

With every wave that tickles land,
A playful spirit does expand.
Joining in the jolly spree,
Life's a canvas, wild and free.

Melody of the Mariner

A sailor sings with a twist of fate,
His boat's a dance, and he's the mate.
With squawking birds and a fishy cheer,
He shouts, 'Yo ho!' to the seagull near.

The waves chuckle as they play along,
A dolphin flips and joins the song.
"Take that, crab!" he laughs in glee,
As it scuttles back to its sanded decree.

The sunset drips like melting cheese,
He dreams of cocktails and ocean breeze.
But all he gets is seaweed stew,
Served with a side of shrimp and goo.

Now off he goes with a wink and a grin,
While the octopus waves, it's time to begin.
A mariner's life, so wild and free,
Except when he trips on a small jellyfish glee.

Sunkissed Secrets

Oh, the sun smiles and winks at us,
While we chase crabs in a sand-filled fuss.
Sandy toes and giggly screams,
Building castles fit for dreams.

A seagull swoops with a cheeky caw,
Stealing fries; oh, what a flaw!
We chase it madly, arms flailing high,
Leaving footprints as it flies by.

Beach balls bounce like wayward thoughts,
While the tide plays tricks that none forgot.
"Watch out!" I yell as the waves take a leap,
Now we're soaked, oh, what a heap!

At dusk we sip from coconut bowls,
Telling stories and sharing our souls.
Laughter echoes against the brightening moon,
Who knew the ocean could echo so soon?

Whispers of the Horizon

A talking parrot recites grand tales,
As sunbeams dance, writing on gales.
"Yo ho, matey!" he squawks with flair,
While we pretend to brush seaweed hair.

The horizon winks, playing peekaboo,
With colors that belong to a daydream hue.
Fish wear shades and boast about their fins,
While turtles tangle in splashy grins.

Here comes the tide, a cheeky old chap,
Tugging our towels—a slippery trap!
We dance and dodge, it's a splashing race,
As crabs chuckle and join the chase.

Evening paints its remarks in gold,
While stories of sea monsters are told.
With a clink of glasses, laughter we cheer,
In this surreal place, we've nothing to fear.

Azure Dreams on Sandy Shores

Under a sky that's way too bright,
We chase shadows that sprout in flight.
With flip-flops flapping, we zoom and sway,
Pretending the beach is our cabaret.

Young pirates digging for sunken treasure,
Find only shells in a measureless pleasure.
"One-eyed Willie" shouts from afar,
"Watch out for crabs that drive fancy cars!"

As seahorses dance in suits so grand,
We sip drinks from the coconut land.
What's in those cups? Who can say?
Just know they add some sway to our play.

At twilight's stage, we celebrate bliss,
Kissing the stars, oh, how could we miss?
With giggles and hiccups, we end our spree,
Thanking the ocean for its laughter spree.

Gentle Ripples of Tomorrow

Waves are wiggling, dancing round,
The fish wear hats, have party sounds.
Driftwood floats with a cheeky grin,
As crabs compete to see who'll win.

Sunshine giggles, making a fuss,
Seashells chatter, who rides the bus?
Palm trees sway with an awkward twist,
With coconut dreams that can't be missed.

Laughter bubbles from the deep blue,
Octopuses playing peek-a-boo.
A parrot's joke just hit the mark,
As dolphins dance and leave a spark.

Tomorrow's breeze will blow us fun,
In a world where we all are one.
With silly tides and wavy plays,
We'll greet the dawn in joyful ways.

Saffron Dusk Over Warm Waters

Saffron skies do silly things,
As pelicans pretend to sing.
Seas shimmer like a disco ball,
While sunsets make the seabirds call.

The boats are bobbing up and down,
As laughter floats beyond the town.
A crab dressed up in fancy clothes,
Stole the show, that everyone knows.

Fish in pajamas swim about,
While turtles join the fun, no doubt.
Chasing shadows, making friends,
This playful dusk never ends.

With slime and giggles, joy bestowed,
Each wave a secret, fun overload.
As colors blend in a comic way,
Tomorrow brings another play.

Glimmers of Hopes and Horizons

The sun is grinning on the shore,
While seagulls peek and laugh for more.
Waves bounce high, a comedic feat,
As sandcastles accept defeat.

The horizon stretches with a wink,
Where mermaids gather on the brink.
With sparkly tales of wacky lore,
They share their laughs, and then explore.

Tiny crabs tap-dance on the sand,
In bright outfits, their own brand.
Anemones sway to their sweet tunes,
While jellyfish wiggle under moons.

With glimmers bright, a playful race,
The ocean's humor knows no space.
In this joyful realm, smiles ignite,
And every wave brings pure delight.

Flight of the Parrots

Parrots squawking with flair,
Wings like disco balls in air,
Bright feathers tossing around,
In this madcap jungle sound.

A toucan with a goofy grin,
Takes a dive, forgets to spin,
Lands a beak's breadth from a tree,
Laughing at its own mischief spree.

Balloons of colors aplenty,
Racing clouds, oh so dainty!
Chasing tails of playful mist,
In the sky, they twist and twist.

Soaring high with giggles loud,
Making mischief, feeling proud.
Nature's jesters on full display,
Who knew birds could be this way?

Dancing Shadows Over Sand

Footprints traced in sugar grains,
The sun's hot tango, it explains.
Crabs in costumes, quite absurd,
Wobble sideways, never heard.

Kites above play peek-a-boo,
With kids who dance like they're brand new,
Belly flops make waves hiss and pop,
Noses dive, then they plop!

A coconut rolls, steals the show,
Chasing laughter as it goes slow,
Shells giggle, whispering their tales,
While seaweed dons its fancy trails.

Sunset paints a canvas bright,
As shadows plot their next delight.
Dancing wildly, oh so grand,
On the twinkling golden sand.

Beyond the Coral Veil

Bubbles rise in silly glee,
Fish in masks sip cups of tea,
Seahorses waltz, swaying by,
In this underwater high-five!

Starfish hold a talent show,
With jellyfish performing a flow,
A crab cracks jokes, oh so punny,
Their antics worth a heap of money!

Corals paint all shades of cheer,
Pirates laugh, but have no fear,
Treasure maps drawn on the sand,
X marks the giggle, not the grand.

Behind each wave, a chuckle hides,
With surfboards riding funny tides.
Beneath this veil of colors bright,
Jokes collide in pure delight.

Radiant Horizons

Sticky fingers reach for the sky,
With popsicles that never die,
Sunburnt noses make summer sings,
As laughter dances on warm wings.

A hammock swings with sleepy tunes,
While fruit bats twirl under moons,
Bananas make for goofy hats,
Running 'round with crazy bats!

Fuzzy clouds play hide and seek,
While kids on surfboards squeal and squeak,
Chasing rainbows, silly and bold,
With tales of laughter to be told.

Horizons burst with colors vast,
Time rolls on, we've made a blast,
As night falls in a bubble of fun,
Tomorrow's laughter just begun!

Lullabies of the Lagoon

In waters where the crabs do dance,
A fish wears goggles, taking a chance.
The lilies giggle under the sun,
While turtles compete in a laughing run.

A frog croaks tunes, quite out of tune,
Splashing around like a jaunty cartoon.
With dragonflies flitting, making a fuss,
As they dodge the snickers of a sneaky bus.

A hermit crab grumbles, stuck in his shell,
Comically puffing like he's casting a spell.
While the sun sets low, the colors swirl bright,
With laughter and bubbles, we dance through the night.

Oh, the lagoon's lullabies make us all cheer,
With each silly joke, we forget all our fear.
Bubbles and giggles, a joyous display,
Join in the chorus of this playful ballet.

Indigo Bounty

In waters so deep, where the mermaids play,
They always have snacks for a lunchtime buffet.
A parrot pretends to be a seabird sage,
While the fish flip-flop, like they're on a stage.

The seaweed giggles, tickling the toes,
While starfish applaud, striking their pose.
An octopus juggles sea shells with flair,
While a clam shouts jokes, without any care.

Crabs in a conga, kicking up sand,
Banana peels fly by, isn't life grand?
With each playful splash, we're riding the wave,
In a bustling ocean, we're all pretty brave.

So if you are hungry for laughter and fun,
Dive into the blue where we laugh and we run.
With treasures aplenty and friends all around,
In the indigo bounty, joy knows no bound!

Canopy of Stars

Under a blanket of twinkling light,
The owls tell tales that tickle our fright.
A raccoon plays chess with a curious fox,
While fireflies buzz like curious clocks.

The branches sway gently, a rhythm divine,
A squirrel in slippers calls it design.
He hosts a grand party for all woodland folks,
While old trees chuckle at their silly jokes.

The moon spills secrets with magical gleam,
While hedgehogs hum softly, lost in a dream.
They dance with the shadows, no care for the time,
A whimsical waltz, a tune so sublime.

Amongst all the laughter, forget all your woes,
In this canopy world, anything goes.
With clouds as our pillows and stars as our guide,
Let's giggle and sing till the morning tide!

Seaglass Symphony

On shores where the gulls make a ruckus and din,
A treasure of glass is waiting to win.
They clink and they jingle, a merry brigade,
While sandcastles sprout like a dizzy charade.

A crab in a tux does a pirouette,
With shells as his partners, a sight to be met.
The tide hums along, a melodious tune,
As starfish join in, under the light of the moon.

The beach ball rolls in on the waves with a flair,
Where pint-sized pirates are chasing a pair.
With flip-flops a-clapping, and laughter abound,
Every grain of sand shakes to the sound.

So stride on the shoreline, joyous and free,
In a seaglass symphony, let's just be glee.
With the ocean as our stage, we'll never miss,
The funny little moments, wrapped up in bliss!

Hibiscus Whispers

In a garden where colors clash,
Petals gossip in a sassy flash.
Birds wear hats that look absurd,
They chirp in rhythm, oh, how they're heard.

Sunlight pours like laughter bright,
Bees dance around, oh what a sight!
Sipping nectar, they make a toast,
To all the flowers they love the most.

Breezes play tricks on my hat,
As I chase it down—oh, how about that!
Nature's comedy, laughing aloud,
In this lively, vibrant crowd.

With every breeze, a new surprise,
A mirthful breeze, a bouncing prize.
So here we giggle, tease and sway,
In this earthly ballet, come what may.

Between the Canopies and the Blue

In jungle gyms of leafy green,
Monkeys swing on ropes unseen.
They throw coconuts in a game,
Yelling 'Heads up!'—it's all the same.

Alligators bask with nonchalant flair,
Pretending they're sofas, oh, what a pair!
While parrots chat with gossip and glee,
They squawk, 'You won't believe what I see!'

Sunglasses on, the world they view,
They flip and dive into waters blue.
Splashing around like they own the place,
Oh dear, that fish—what a funny face!

With laughter echoing through the trees,
Nature's jesters, they aim to please.
So take a peek between each hue,
For chuckles aplenty are waiting for you.

Dreamscapes of Serene Waters

Floating on waves like a fluffy dream,
A fisherman spills his fishy scheme.
He plans to catch some goldfish grand,
But winds up with seaweed in his hand.

Gulls cackle as they dive for a snack,
Swooping down—there's no looking back!
They steal a sandwich, then make a fuss,
Polishing off crumbs without much fuss.

Underwater, a crab shows off,
Some dance moves that make you scoff.
He claps his claws to the ocean's beat,
Crowning himself as king of the street!

Rippling laughter, the tides do sing,
With every splash, the joy takes wing.
So dive into fun, let worries cease,
For in these waters, we find our peace.

The Lure of Distant Horizons

Far away, where dreams come alive,
A pirate parrot plans to thrive.
He maps a path to buried delight,
But ends up lost in a mango flight.

With treasure chests filled up with sand,
He declares himself the captain of the land.
Fish wear crowns, and crabs salute,
As seashells giggle in their loot.

Waves tease and pull, a merry chase,
The horizon blushes, what a face!
Surfboards riding, giggling high,
As sun touches down, painting the sky.

So come aboard this laughter spree,
With tales of winds and salty glee.
Adventure calls from afar, it's true,
In this wide, wild world, there's fun for you.

Sunlit Canopy

Beneath the green, a parrot squawks,
While monkeys trade their silly socks.
A coconut drops with a thud so loud,
I laugh alone, a merry crowd.

The light dances on leaves so bright,
Suntanned lizards bask in delight.
Each breeze brings whispers, funny tales,
Of sunburned tourists who forgot their gales.

Pineapple hats and umbrella drinks,
As gulls look down and give us winks.
A limbo contest breaks the heat,
The champion? A turtle who can't keep his feet!

So join the fun, let worries flee,
In a world so wild, just let it be.
With laughter echoing through the land,
We'll dance amidst the grains of sand.

Waves of Desire

Under a sun that likes to tease,
I chase my hat, blown by a breeze.
I dive for treasures, or so I think,
Only to find a fish that can wink.

With surfboards dancing, all in a row,
I try to catch waves, but hey, whoa!
I wipe out big, in a splash of foam,
Caught by a crab who's claiming his home.

Seagulls squawk, giving me looks,
As I search for shells like ancient books.
The tide rolls in with a giggle and swirl,
And suddenly seaweed becomes my new curl!

Waves laugh back with a playful nudge,
As I finally sit back and won't budge.
With salty kisses on my cheek,
I'll keep this joy all the week.

Lost in Azure Dreams

In a hammock strung between two trees,
I dream of fish that smile with ease.
Palm leaves rustle, with rhythms divine,
As I ponder life over a glass of brine.

The sky winks down in playful glee,
While I float along, just me and the sea.
Jellyfish dance to waves of delight,
I think they've been sipping drinks all night!

Driftwood castles rise and fall,
Handmade kingdoms that aren't too tall.
Sandy moats filled with seaweed treasure,
Only found in dreams of pure pleasure.

Yet here in this bliss, I find it absurd,
That every wave feels like a word.
So I sip my thoughts beneath the gleam,
And let my worries drift with the stream.

Dappled Light and Laughter

With laughter scattered through the trees,
Nature's giggle flows with the breeze.
Sunlight dapples in a playful tease,
As I chase laughter, just like a sneeze.

Frogs wear crowns made of shiny leaves,
While I try not to trip on bee's reveries.
A butterfly lands with a silken bow,
Mimicking dancers who twist and throw.

Picnic spread with crumbs galore,
Ants audition for a dance floor.
Picnic blankets and funny hats,
Join in the fun — hey, look at that!

So gather round and join the cheer,
The world is wacky but oh so dear.
With dappled light shining bright and bold,
We'll write our stories, both funny and gold.

Rhythms of the Tides

The waves are dancing, oh so spry,
Like fish in tuxedos, they flip and fly.
Seagulls are laughing, grace in their dives,
Who knew that fish could mimic jive?

The beach ball bounced, it snatched a cap,
A hungry crab shouted, "Hey, a snack!"
While teens in shades chase after their fries,
Sand castles crumble, to everyone's surprise!

The sun wears shades, what a sight to see,
As flip-flops squeak a symphony.
Beach towels buzzing, they squabble and chat,
While sunscreen bottles join in – how about that?

With oceanic antics, laughter flows free,
Who knew that seaweed could twirl with glee?
A dolphin swung by with a wink and a flip,
As beachgoers cheered with a triumphant skip!

Where the Sun Meets the Ocean

A fluffy cloud pranced on the edge of day,
While sailboats giggled, 'We're on our way!'
The sun dropped low, with a wink and a shout,
Seashells convened to join in the bout.

The horizon painted a mess of bright hues,
As a crab with shades strutted, 'I've got the moves!'
Lively coconuts joined the fun on the shore,
While waves said, 'We've danced enough, let's do more!'

Sun-kissed smiles and laughter in air,
Flying fish flopped like they just didn't care.
And as the sun slipped from a lacquered throne,
A parrot squawked, 'This crown is my own!'

With every splash, joy takes a flight,
While flip-flops flip in the fading light.
Sand between toes, happiness is near,
And the moon laughed back, 'What a fun-filled sphere!'

Twilight Undercanopies

In the hush of dusk, critters come alive,
A squirrel in shades attempts a cool jive.
Fireflies twinkle like stars on a spree,
While turtles debate on who gets to be free.

The palm fronds whisper secrets and dreams,
As the sea chuckles, 'Ain't this as it seems?'
The breeze tickles noses; oh what a delight!
As shadowy antics paint magic by night.

Crickets compose symphonies so grand,
While iguanas prance, forming a band.
Every wave carries echoes of glee,
With laughter bouncing like balls down the spree.

Under the twilight, the tales intertwine,
As every creature performs its own sign.
And if you listen, you might hear a cheer,
From the ocean and forest, in camaraderie clear!

Mosaics of Mango and Melodies

Mangoes are tumbling, a colorful sight,
As monkeys in trees have a fruit-fueled fight.
Juice drips like laughter, sticky and sweet,
While parrots squawk songs to the tropical beat.

A picnic arrives with sandwiches galore,
Ants march along like they've found a store.
'Who needs a table? We've got our own stage,'
As the watermelon rolls into a rage!

The sun dips low, painting colors anew,
While coconut shakers add flair to the crew.
Bananas all giggle, as laughter and cheer,
Spread like confetti in this fruity frontier.

As night blankets softly with twinkling glow,
The melodies linger, as breezes bestow.
In the land of delight, where joy takes its flight,
Every bite, every laugh, is a festival bright!

www.ingramcontent.com/pod-product-compliance
Lightning Source LLC
Chambersburg PA
CBHW072220070526
44585CB00015B/1429